NOTHING BUT THE RAIN
A COLLECTION OF POEMS

PHEN WESTON

Copyright © 2014 Phen Weston

Cover Photo © 2012 Willow Stancombe

All rights reserved.

All images within used with permission

or found in the public domain.

darknesswarmth.wordpress.com/

Twitter: @phenweston

Facebook: www.facebook.com/youmustsuffermetogomyowndarkway

ISBN: 150109162X
ISBN-13: 978-1501091629

FOR WILLOW

You give me unconditional love and support always, making me stronger each day. Our adventures are endless and flawless.

Contents

A Few Thoughts ix

5am 11

Willow Sheltered Shores 12

Aphrodisia 15

Sounding Out P. 19

Soul In A Wallet 21

Nothing But The Rain 22

Just Another Night 23

Blues 27

Today I Will. 29

Shooting Stars And Nightscapes 30

H + D x Y = C 31

Her Ghost Walks Stars 32

I, Dummy 34

Words Drawn 36

What Holds An Old Photograph? 37

You Danced In The Forest 39

Xyst 41

Tupperware Trepidation 43

Stop Where We Left Off 44

On A Hill We Rest 46

Concrete Plastic Memory 47

Her Seppuku 49

Another 5am 51

Beckons The Breach 53

The Wordsmith 55

The Hummingbird's Song 57

Cadaverous Funfair 58

Microscopic Macrocosm 59

Atrabilious Ataraxia 61

Today Tumbled 62

The Clouds Of North Holland 64

Watersmeet 65

Vexation Lulls Him 68

Journey Of An Ancient Pebble 69

Xian 70

Thoughts On Gods 73

Awaiting What Comes 75

Nonsense… 77

Without A Footprint 78

Defibrillated Love 80

To W. 81

Pont de l'Archevêché 83

Can We Sail Away? 85

The Victorian Portrait Company 86

The Worlds We Create 87

The Eve Of War 89

The Empath 91

Tao 93

Sleep Grimalkin 95

4am (The Prequel) 100

A Few Thoughts

This is the provocative thoughts, feelings, people, places and events within my life in 2014. This is not to say that all the poems contained here are a reflection of real life, as you shall see, but more a reflection of my world, sanity, insanity, thoughts. In these pages I have strived to connect to life through words. To grasp the realities, both beautiful and harsh, of everything about me. Or maybe these words are just etched into the universe for fun? This collection, the stories, images, meanings, ignorances, are all me, laid out and exposed.

I could not have got this far without needing to thank a few people. So I would like to do that here. Thank you! To my parents, Pam and Fraser. My wonderful brother Nicholas. Thank you to Lucia and Kieron, the soon to be in-laws, for putting up with me and allowing me to marry their daughter! To my friends, who I love dearly and to the amazing community of writers and bloggers I have come to know, respect and love at WordPress, who, over the last few months, have encouraged and inspired me beyond anything I could ever envisage!

Most of all I would like to say thank you to the one this book is dedicated to, Willow. You are a star brighter than any other, constantly guiding and supporting. I could never have done this without you.

So without further interruption. Please enjoy and I hope you find some words to inspire you. For more of me please visit my blog at:

http://darknesswarmth.wordpress.com/

Regards,
Phen

PHEN WESTON

5am

"Tread softly because you tread on my dreams."
- William Butler Yeats

Sky aflame

With vermillion passion

Adrift

Empty streets

Silently serenade

Silken

Within my pocket

Hemingway hums

Static.

Willow Sheltered Shores

"Every life is a march from innocence, through temptation, to virtue or vice."
- Lyman Abbott

How did the turning tides
Save such graceful folly?
I was once a child
Playing at
The false man.

Who knew such belongings?
That the truest love
Could blend
The margins of life
Into forgotten wants.

I tried to be a man
Before the child,
Giving to one the world
With every fibre,
Returned woefully nought.

And all that could fill
The annihilation
Left by such softly
Spoken poison,

NOTHING BUT THE RAIN

A child man deformed

How could I not hurt next
When through such beauty
Lay innocence seraph?
In form elegantly formed,
A pedestal told unreachable.

Deformed, I could not climb
To such a dizzying high
With childish grip
And weakened woes,
Only topple, neanderthalesqeue.

Yet all that toppled
Was innocence chambered,
My heart, the mirror obscured
Into one hundred thousand
Beads of splintered fate.

Heartbreak self-inflicted,
Irrational barricades repeated,
The Winchester bites sharp,
Guilt cried deathly hallows,
Children's innocence passes on.

Into darkness crawled,
Blinded by such forfeiture,
I betrayed compassion's

Passive place for me
In this hollow world.

Near the dark half cowered,
And the black became god,
Until your exquisite light
Resonated, instigating form
Anew, my holy potter.

Each smile embraced
With harmonious eyes,
Flourishes and nourishment,
Changed, altered, transformed
Through your grace and love.

Innocence taken
Does not pay for
Innocence taken,
But through lost innocence
We transform,
Beautifully, wonderfully.

To find a path given
With such significance,
Enchantress of my heart
Your love guided me to
Willow sheltered shores.

Aphrodisia

*"There are mysteries which men can only guess
at, which age by age they may solve only in part."*
- Bram Stoker

What is the measure of life
But the distance travelled
From womb to catacomb,
Does the ever after take account?

For my abominable sins
Turbulent rest undermines
My once human animation,
Foreshadowing my tomb.

In life the devil made work
For these idle hands, cravings,
Depravity bound hand in hand,
Her name ravenous Aphrodisia.

But was my sinning greater
Than those whose lives since
I have claimed in her hungry call,
Through, desire, hand and teeth?

From crypt to cryptic existence
Life began, a long time since

The sorrow of concluded days
Never meant for human ways.

Once I waited with anguish for death,
While now all I covert is strange fate
To guide my cold steady gaze
From this doom that binds me.

My first blood wept between
The veil of time's gentle touch,
Blissfully widowed she claimed,
A murderer for profit she laid.

I honed my forsaken inflicted kiss
Only feeding on those damned
By their own hateful desires,
Sin tastes sweet when caught fresh.

Tranquility came after thirst,
Addictive struggle taking the place
Of any hope and lost humanity
That may still crawl in twilight.

Each one after, deep longing,
Grew stronger within, until
I could not fight the animalistic
Nature of the devil I had become.

On blood dyed days my heart

NOTHING BUT THE RAIN

Lay entombed by a nature
I could never hope to end,
Damned I wandered evermore.

Strange decades twinned
Stranger centuries, each day
Never ending, never more.
Who was I now in dark minds?

I moved between the worlds
A figment, spectre of the night,
Ashamed of the devil within,
No longer a man without.

Long days I searched the world,
Across the sands of decay,
And never lingered a thread
Of embraced divinity, Aphrodisia.

We yearned for each other
But beast enough I'd never be,
She was queen of deformity,
Humanity flooded my veins.

Centuries became repentant love
The sins of man and monster,
All for a devotion I would never know
Forever I crawled alone.

Why were two hearts enriched
Through rapture and infatuation
Never to know more than a brief kiss
That engulfed, killed and condemned.

Love's totality traced our worlds,
Linked with the putrid darkness
That we had longingly become,
Children of such nights.

Sometimes I pray for death
To stop the hunger in my breast,
But never does its kiss relieve
Or relinquish dusk's torment.

Aphrodisia my queen of sorrow,
How you damned each tomorrow,
With what could never be,
Is my sin enough for thee?

What is the measure of life
But the distance travelled
From womb to catacomb,
Does the ever after take account?

Sounding Out P.

*"Painting is silent poetry, and poetry is painting
with the gift of speech."*
- Simonides

Pixelated images

Dance across the carpet,

Perhaps today

Will wish the world anew,

Preparing tomorrow

For adventures too few,

Prevised realism

In great years to come,

Precious postures

Sweep into daze ahead,

Playfully wishing

For fears to be shed,

Passion out plays

Within strange forgiveness,

Poignant meanderings

Blessed to those who catch,

Prosperous thoughts

Formed, never to detach,

Photogenic images,

Words blended triumphantly,

Pleasantly,

Pleasingly,

Peacefully.

Soul In A Wallet

I keep your soul
In my ageing wallet,

A faded photograph
Of a Paris affiance,

Dated train tickets
To love's journey's past,

Pebbles and sharks' teeth,
Perforated thoughts,

A menagerie of receipts
Not for returns, but reminders,

I keep your soul
In my ageing wallet,

The unimportant stuff
(Money, cards, coins)

Stay loose in my pocket,
A place as fickle as they.

Nothing But The Rain

Through life's chaos

Did she die grounded?

He promised ardor,

Asking only what she saw

Before the fading light

Of elapsed finite presence,

"Nothing but the rain"

She sincerely appealed,

Falling through the universe,

Spiraling star that she was,

The cooling eternal winds

Filled her earthly lungs,

Every movement reverberated

Creation's cosmic waltz,

Her eyes saw wonders

Beyond human comprehension,

And she lived again… again… again…

"What do you see my love?"

"Nothing but the rain".

NOTHING BUT THE RAIN

PHEN WESTON

Just Another Night

The night, cold and silent,
Held a warmth and sound
That echoed through my thoughts.
It wasn't deafening as it crashed
All around, only mildly amusing.
The shadows devoured the light
Which gracefully enhanced
Their deep rich darkness.
The world circled and danced,
Leapt and ran, swimming
Throughout the witching hour.

The cat materialised before me.
Its enchanted song held my heart
As his eyes spoke of all the dreams
That were still to dream,
All the worlds that were to be created
His hypnotic stare echoed
In the heavens. Each star
Performing its personal ballet,
A perfect balance of nature
And the sublime
"Wordsworth" the Cat spoke

"Is my name" with a smile
Of darkest delight dashed

NOTHING BUT THE RAIN

With a cherry. "We've met before"
I stood and stared sadly down;
How could I have met him before?
More importantly how could I forget?
Assuming that was the key
To this whole state of affairs.
He stood on his back paws,
Omnipotent, omniscient, omnibenevolent.
"I am the lamb and the Tyger."

My eyes blankly looked through
Him to an untamed realm beyond,
Could anything we wanted be possible there?
If this were true, why Wordsworth?
So I asked,
"Why Wordsworth?"
Overhead, the stars danced their waltz of creation.
In the distance thunder flashed fussily
Demanding attention from a situation
They couldn't understand.
Heck! I couldn't for that matter.

"The night runs wild with the sublime.
It wasn't a physical choice
Maybe a metaphysical one?
He understood the secret.
Through words that only Wordsworth
Could weave you, and many more,
Understood what I am,"

He sniffed the air coldly,
Around him his translucent fur
Shifted colours and shades.
He sniffed the air warmly.

"Are you god?"
Serenity eased my soul
Surprisingly the stars sort satisfaction,
Pleasingly passing through philosophies
That Homo sapiens were not ready to understand.
"I am what you want.
What hold you to good
And nature. The sublime
That shakes your foundation
And allows you to see the sugariness
That is always around you. That and more".

All at once it came to me,
I too was omniscient.
The universe that sang
To the soul swam deep within,
Like it does for all those who listen.
With that the Cat stepped back
Deep into the satirical shadows
Gently purring pragmatically, gone.
For a minute I stood staring
Into the empty spaces of the sphere.
I was late for work.

Blues

"They hear it come out, but they don't know how it got there. They don't understand that's life's way of talking. You don't sing to feel better. You sing 'cause that's a way of understanding life."
- Ma Rainey

Tarmac tears
    Running red lights,
Nothing for tonight,
    Just blinking dead lights,
When I see you,
    The summer dress
Blowing in sour winds,
    I remember the blues
Are here to stay,
    Never the other way,
Life's always on delay,
    Lies and tiaras,
The stuttering repeat
    Of another failed day,
A a a again…
    Twilight comes,
The lonely drum
    Rat-a-tat-tats, Beat
On moody blues

    Against soul and body,
The synchronised
    Etched notes of
Never more, sudden
    Haulage of hidden rain
Filling empty streets,
    Tussle of torn lovers,
Could the beat sound
    For us? Would the echo
Cease with us?
    Discover me when
You search for you today,
    I may be there, cold disparity,
Then maybe we could
    Sing the blues away.

Today I Will...

Today
I
will
hold
you
collide, as
may though
worlds

skies may ignite,

god
wept
from
solitude,

as though you
have never been
by my side,

because
the
universe
lies
about
forever.

PHEN WESTON

Shooting Stars And Nightscapes

Shooting stars and nightscapes

Filled a warm summer night,

We sat, softly stirring, sentient,

Blessed to be wholly in sync,

Our journey would soon begin,

Yet, in the great scale of existent,

It would end even faster,

Eyes locked, lips sealed,

Hearts convulsing at one million

Beats per minute, until…

Suns go supernova with

A galaxy driven serenade,

Planets pulse with life,

Love, an endless cacophony

Of hopes and dreams,

Soon to suffer the ravages

Of infinite time, turning

To dust, heavenly stardust,

Crumbling, engulfing, drowned

In the black hole of all there is.

Reborn, remerging, romancing forever,

I look into your eyes and know,

For now, you are all the universe I need.

H + D x Y = C

Show me why
I shouldn't stay,
When we would
Shift and merge
Through each day,
And all the whose
We could become
Play out through
Our unknown sum
Of hopes and dreams
Until we are complete,
A vestige suffuse with
Labyrinthine memories,
We wrap the senses,
A lagoon of feelings
Lithe in your arms,
You are the sum
Of all that I will be,
And in your soft
Graceful arms
I find my eternity.

Her Ghost Walks Stars

Through births and deaths,

Haunting oceans of emptiness,

She solely walks with

Universal falling stars,

An apparition to dead worlds

Manifested between nebulous crypts,

As revenant watcher of long days

She wistfully travelled light years,

A spiraling impression

Faintly touching those who lived

Grounded, A trace, hint, suggestion

Of what could have been,

And all she yearned, the one

Who sent her pirouetting

Through the heavens, false love,

Breathless she had become,

Black hole and doppelgänger,

Reformed and deformed,

Invisible to all who could have

Changed her failing orbit,

How could she not become

The fault in her own star?

When her internal reflection paled

Against the backdrop of the universe,

Macrocosms revolved, Totality embraced,

She became endless cosmic dust

Floating through outer space,

Atoms split, timelessly out of place…

I, Dummy

Marionette sketches

Reflected through

Rear view mirrors,

Screaming at me

The used-to-bes.

Your fingers caressed

My strings, subtly

Stroked my firm

Wooden frame,

Oak backbone quivered,

I thought I could be

A real boy, thought

I could know real joy

It was all for nought,

What I sought in you

Was not the enchanted

World you dangled before

Me, through each twitch

Of your extremities

A frigid tactile part of me

Is harshly dismembered,

Am I responsible

For my heartless mistakes

If behind my scenes

You manipulate

NOTHING BUT THE RAIN

Each and every step I take,

Fantoccini subverted,

Disconcerted exposure

Self-possession nullified,

And yet questionably

The comfort of your fine

Suggestive movements

Fills me with security

And peace of mind,

Is your wielding power

Wholly that bad when fine-spun

Lies hold my plywood

World together,

Inconspicuous,

Penetrating,

Obscure,

And I, too dummy, cannot

Separate my soul from yours,

Scissors blunt

From the strength of your ties,

A wooden doll I will always be,

I dance for you

My sweet manipulator.

PHEN WESTON

Words Drawn

You drew a picture
Of me today,
Surrounded by
The words I tend,

With no surprise,
Each of them
Led back to you,

Your lines, shading
And hue accentuate
The idioms, lexis
And expressions
Of me,

You make I,
Infinite, ongoing,
Tracing the circle
of illustrated us,

What would either be
Without our muse?

What Holds An Old Photograph?

Once there was

An old photograph

That held a world,

Long forgotten

In black and white,

Picturesquely means,

A memory captured,

Now absent of those

Who once gave it life,

What would it be like

To escape into

Your negative view?

A resemblance

Of yesterday, identical

To fictional today,

Angles and proportions,

Thoughts as different

As stray substance,

Once there was

An old photograph

That held a world,

Echoes adrift

On time's lonely

Vanished daze.

You Danced In The Forest

We danced among deafening light,

As blinding thunder buried down

To where the physical lost control,

I watched you twirl, loop, spiral

Like true elegance had been

Your binding wish to hold you

To this figmental holy kingdom,

Each breath you took held such éclat

Meaning to the falling universe,

Who could have seen our days

Were as numbered as a Renoir?

Your brilliance and conspicuous

Nature brightens the storms,

Highlighting your storybook,

I shower you with praise and applause,

Is it what you hear in the forest

When you're naked and alone?

What symbols your heart can bare,

Simply spartan, but full of definition,

Was it psychologically thrilling?

That hopeless feeling comes again

And I am lost without your hands,

How can I hold on to one so dreamlike?

The world cracked, bottom to top,

I lovingly stepped forward,

Ready to drop…

The wind took me away from you,

Draped with fear, waking nightmare,

I lost all sense of who I could become,

Your exuberant hold slipped away,

Irresolute, impulsive, irreconcilable.

Xyst

Tangled transient,

Triple world score!

I walk through the xyst

Of taught unknown

Surreal minds,

Poignantly the mist

Circles my standing,

Cease and desist

With these nightly terrors

When heaven's grace

Kisses the sky,

Enlightenment,

Subtle azures dry

The tears from the eye,

In the shade we sit,

Collected romance

Aided by the years,

Are we once again fit

To be in this garden

Of serenity when,

By its very definition,

Knowledge is sought

Through connected beauty?

Beauty is in my eyes,

Beholder!

Mother's wit,

Snakes and apples

Are a curse to some,

But god does not judge

Those who seek truth,

Only blesses them

With everlasting peace,

When walls of vanity crumble

Along paths who stumbles

Over crack and crevice?

Narrow fissure,

In my mind

I'll glide today

Along your path

And hold tomorrow's light

At bay until I am ready

To stay within its boundless

Dreams, ambitious trace,

Together let us dance

Once more!

Tupperware Trepidation

Tupperware trepidation,
Vacuum sealed for my freshness.
I rush in to the words I write,
With little thought to how they are interpreted.

When I see how happy you are
Confusion's uneasy stare dissolves my composure,
I feel that I am the devil's symphony
Composed by my own idle hands.

When I see how happy you are
I hate that which makes you feel that way
Because I want it to be me!
I should be happy to see you smile.

I rush the words I write
To be certain I cannot concuss my emotions
With the impact of their truths,
You're better off without me!

Tupperware trepidation,
When that lid is lifted for this last time,
There is no putting my defences back in the box.
Influx and influence by my own downfall.

Stop Where We Left Off

Noises

In the dark,

Were we ever

Anything more?

What sensitivity

Are we looking for?

Intensive care

Belongs to other

Beings,

I yield,

I screamed,

I died

Ten thousand times,

For us…

Each beautiful

Without you,

NOTHING BUT THE RAIN

The king of

Forget-me-not

Cleanses

Nothing,

Purifies

Less,

And we?

Extract me

For your equation,

The mathematical

Improbability,

Signatures bare,

Am I worth it?

I never was from the start,

Keep it for someone

Tangled…

PHEN WESTON

On A Hill We Rest

On a hill we rest,

Watching virtue

Hold the heavens,

You say

"Most of those stars

Are already dead,"

Maybe it's morbid curiosity

To stare longingly

Towards them,

Passion and spirit dance,

Skies conserve substance,

And life flows,

Within their depth

There is love eternal,

And I stare…

NOTHING BUT THE RAIN

Concrete Plastic Memory

"Nothing will see us through the age we're entering but high consciousness, and that comes hard. We don't have a good, modern myth yet, and we need one."
- Robert Johnson

He moved into obscurity,
Beyond tempered realities
Of sequestered life,
How were places forgotten?

A wild public domain
Hidden away between
Impossible possibilities,
Beyond buoyancy of mind,

How he got here,
You would never believe,
Such will of conscious,
Off the beaten track,

Here was isolated,
Simply complicated,
A cloister of forever,
Here he should always be,

The grass was greener,

The sky was purer,
Flora and fauna deviated
From concrete, plastic memory,

Which secluded specialty,
The ability of tendency,
Life, ebullience, euphoria
Nature reclaimed his heart,

Moulded reconstruction
Took its rightful place,
The world only god knew,
Moves between sanity,

And what could they expect
When at heart he was nature
In form, even distorted
By concrete, plastic memory,

Nature represented his destiny,
Sculptured secret unfrequented,
Out of the way,
Off the beaten path.

Her Seppuku

The bamboo wife

Saw

The melancholy man

With tombstones

In his eyes,

White ritual

And grey whispers

Soon bloomed,

Turning to clouds,

Soaking the earth,

Splinters

Ran down her cheeks,

Ligneous

Tears of tragedy,

Jagged and ripe,

Regret's demeanour

Could not stand

Between their worlds,

Tormented,

Mourning broke,

She loved him

Once,

Twice,

Into shattered pieces,

She couldn't speak,

Forwards

He fell,

Tantō carved,

Crimson passion,

Love honoured.

NOTHING BUT THE RAIN

PHEN WESTON

Another 5am

The morning still holds nightly shades,

With little vibrancy in pale light,

The air deceivingly seems warm,

But I shiver anyway as I step out

Into the hushed early dawn,

There's a heat wave coming

The wireless claims, a British summer,

Of wants and expectations

That never seem to materialise,

I'll wait and see if their world appears,

The work radio kicks out static and old hits

That should have stayed in their era,

There is no king of rock 'n' roll today,

No melody to revitalise the soul,

While all the time Lovecraft, lurking

In the shadows, haunts my sleepy thoughts,

Are the old ones watching over me?

Then, out of nowhere, Johnny Cash

Belts his troubled tunes across

The tumbling newspaper stacks,

And my morning finally begins.

Beckons The Breach

I have seen you
Conquer worlds,
Through subtle fear
And sickened tears,
Effluent divinity
Whose damnation
Stands before
Gods and devils
In like and kin,
Freely once more
Unto the breach,
How can serenity
Calmly claim their
Childhood breaths
When darkening
Dreams are the fray,
Fall from heaven,
Line by line by line,
Tired of names given
To soulless objects,
The world holds
Promises so cruelly
Sunken by weighted
Manipulations,
Dust to dust,

Do I know these hills?
Such painful hues
Of begotten wounds,
When comes their time
To lay to peaceful rest?
I hold their like no more,
And cry "once more
Unto the breach,
dear friends"
Angels and devils,
Compassion stands
Before almighty god,
The way shows light
To all who seek it.

The Wordsmith

I eat words like they're Scooby snacks,

Devour syllables and synonyms

Like an army of the walking dead,

Hunger binds me to each page

As though Katnis Everdeen plays

Dracula's undead bride, and the words

Are ever in my favour, 100% pure,

If Walter White taught English

Instead of science, I'd be addicted

To twenty six grams of blue sky

Alphabet, flying high on verse

And crystal clear Shakespeare,

Words smith the mind into the tools

Of the immeasurable imagination,

Romancing the stones outta me,

Definition, preposition, collocation,

A soul without fluidity negates the passion

Fused with Wordsworth's Daffodils

Each sentence a full gun salute

To every tingling thing that makes

Me whole, wrapping words around

The webbed weaving womb of the mind

Marinates senses, sensual, seductive,

A mistress of words seduces the soul

Dexterous manifestation oozes dictation,

Poets fill chasms through emotive longing,

Writers paint the world across the page,

Each sentence creates life, mother, father,

God, I am lost to your wordsmith's way

And who would want it any other way?

The Hummingbird's Song

Each cobalt tear distorts another day,
Equal measures between empty spaces,
Each moment disfigured desire and whim,
The lover waiting for whom the bell tolls,

Can I find your warmth? Among the stars
I open my lines for you to flow through
The breaks of me, each stanza mirrors
The heart that seals sentence and syllable,

Simple words sustain our aching souls,
Am I within your diction? An expression
Of sapphire dreams, a hummingbird
Between our worlds holds our lullaby.

Cadaverous Funfair

All the words fade

And life's an arcade.

Neon lights glare.

Auditory nuisance

Flood the senses,

Masking defences.

Cadaverous funfair

Of decrepit destruction.

I try to find the place

Hidden for me,

Clandestine as it may be.

Radical reconstruction

Of soul sums up

This charlatan's only hope.

Will I succeed?

Will sanity recede?

Only living holds the key.

But who will hold

Me?

Microscopic Macrocosm

It seemed so alien,
Renegade from experience,
A dimensional crossover
Cocooned in the unknown,
That she could love me!
Genuinely care for me!

Without manipulation,
Absent of betrayal,
Concentrated passions
No longer focused fear,
Existence is now measurable
By these new equations.

Microscopic macrocosm
That Mirrors my soul,
Shaped by a thousand years
Of solitude, bullets sweated,
Soulless subjugation of me!
These all implode with her touch,
My forlorn universe goes supernova.

And we live,

And we love,

Kiss, hold, hope, LOVE,

Heaven is at our reach,

Selfish, selfless, surreptitious

Extravagance births a new forever.

Atrabilious Ataraxia

Consumed fiction becomes
The facts of lingering souls,
Regret lies to innocent truth,
Manifesting within complexity,
Intricate refined interactions,
Where does darkness dwell
When acolytes come all at once?
Affable affinity to hidden rooms,
Where all alone, we stand together,
Am I my own antilogy?
The autodidactic anthology
Of contradictions, blue prints
That house idea over matter,
And what does matter
In a world of decadence?
Atrabilious ataraxia,
Sometimes peace is found
In those melancholy moments.

Today Tumbled

Today tumbled

Towards tomorrow

Yearningly yesterday yields,

Forgotten by the young,

Craved by the old,

Yesterday encompasses

The dreams of eternity,

Memories fall through the cracks,

Slip the mind of the masses,

The good, the bad, the ugly,

Past recollections unrivalled,

Seasons surrender to the tempo

Of time's gentle drum,

Acronical kisses

I will not forget you.

Memories of you last

Throughout my lifetime,

Each tender touch,

Every craved kiss,

My epoch absolute.

NOTHING BUT THE RAIN

Aeons skip circumstance,
Pivotal to who we are,
Yet you remain my confidant
A journal in flesh of my rights
And wrongs, requiem and elegy.

Plaintive poet of my soul,
Through melancholy and
Merriment, serenity is my heart,
You are my piece of mind,
And I will not forget you.

The Clouds Of North Holland

The mountainous clouds
Engulfed the landscape,
Rolling through town and countryside.
Maybe it was the beautifully
Formed recumbent land
That gave them their almighty
Grandeur, or maybe,
The elegantly symbolic
Lines that mark and merge
Across each and every pass
Of a landscape enriched
By the cold North Sea.
But inside they conjure
Illusions of long lost kingdoms
Whose vast and ostentatious
Armies would soon undulate
Across the kingdom of my imagination.
Vast battles between raging gods
Of ancient unspoiled waters,
Lir, Poseidon, Nehalennia,
Their uncontrolled passions
Romancing the hearts
Of writers and poets in ways
Jealous to their perception.
Such heavenly nebulosity,
Oh to see and drown again
In your perfect magnificence.

NOTHING BUT THE RAIN

PHEN WESTON

Watersmeet

"All along the valley, stream that flashest white,
Deepening thy voice with the deepening of the night."
- Alfred Lord Tennyson

Fast flowing rivers

Dancing, crossing paths,

Inspiring those whose energy

Beats with your heart,

Shelley walked along

Your churning paths,

Through your eyes

He romanced us all!

Inside you arise

Emotions of peace,

Soft and alluring,

Perfect plentiful ripples

Of passions enhance

The music of the soul,

A meeting of poetical themes,

The sublime, echoes

Of power and ascendance,

Shaking souls on stormy days,

Beauty, when the sun shines

High your gentle voices

Babbles soft serenades of grace,

Now I walk your shores,

Your influence touches,

NOTHING BUT THE RAIN

And through you

Words mimic your waters

And I am inspired!

For centuries you have ebbed

Your way to the sea,

For greater aeons

Your symphony will cascade on,

To bring nature and beauty

To all that cross your ways.

Vexation Lulls Him

She cut the silence
With the desolate knife,
Not hearing
The deafening plea
From his sorrowful abyss,
She never hears
The screaming stillness,
That reserve of
Uncommunicativeness,
His synonym of
All that he hopes for,
But is never fulfilled,

                                                Diffidence, hesitancy,
                                                Reluctance censors
                                                The dreams of their
                                                Togetherness,
                                                He plagues her
                                                With soft saturninity,
                                                Hush solemn silence,
                                                Sleep deathlike silence,
                                                Hold your tongue
                                                One more night.
                                                Subverted downfall,
                                                Let's sing the blues away.

Journey Of An Ancient Pebble

The ancient pebble
Travelled from its ancient
Hindu home with the man
Who came and loved
The ruins of Mỹ Sơn,
Its home for seventeen
Long centuries,
It wanted adventure,
To feel the world's
Presence, to lie and bask
In unknown suns with one
Who thought it eternally more
Than just a pebble at some
Ancient ruins, forgotten
For four hundred years
Was no place for a life
That was built for the worship
Of the humble divine.
Always with the man, it felt
The love of worlds,
Travelled the green fields
Of England, scorched in deserts
Of Africa and journeyed
Along route sixty six,
So much it saw and knew,

All the while loved, felt

And respected by the

One who heeded its call.

Eventually the man grew old

And like so many before

That the stone had known

He faded from the world,

The pebble mourned this life

More than any before or any again,

Blessed with children and grandchildren

Who knew the ancient story

Or their old man's ancient stone,

They journeyed back to fulfil

His dying wish, returning the pebble

With love and care.

Home at last the stone rested

As life passed by, men came

And went, never feeling

The connection that urged

Them for adventure.

It knew though that one day

The world would be seen again,

But for now, it slept.

Xian

"To the mind that is still, the whole universe surrenders."
- Lao Tzu

I stood among
The hanging trees,
Each hanging fruit
Manifested destiny,
Ready for its time
To ripen in the sun,

Upon the hill
Sits an old, old temple,
Flutters of the womb,
Resembled
In the longing
Of its ancient
Wooden tomb,

The temple exists
Before language
And definition,
Before gods and Gia,
Before all the worlds
Of man were thought
Into their existence,

PHEN WESTON

Who am I to gaze
Upon its holy walls,
Vermillion paths
Lined with golden
Faith, blazing
As the eternal one,

I stood among
The hanging trees,
Each hanging fruit
Manifests destiny,
Ascension,
My turn comes
To walk their world,

I stood among
The hanging trees,
Fruit and bounty
Ready to feed,
Nourishing
Enlightenment.

Thoughts On Gods

Rain drops in reverse,

God cried so much for man

That all the oceans couldn't hold

Once spectacular cascades,

They all talk with holy aegis,

But the devil can quote scripture

From back to front, front to back,

Inside, outside, backside,

With sacred claims of dignity

Toxic prophets surrender

Only themselves to devout hate,

Standing on blood-stained blade

Of their own pious knives,

Carriers of ancient star dust,

If gods exist, in any form,

Name, shape, they forgive all

That's done by humans' limited

Understanding

Of universal existence,

Old men forget

Human eyes are young

When perceiving

The beautiful mysteries

That forge existence,

They will see, understand, feel,

The vengeful furry of their gods,

As each sin is forgiven, absolved,

Pardoned, and true love

Fills their soul with peace,

Comprehension, meaning,

Gods forgive all, when all is god.

Awaiting What Comes

The road is long,

Revelations grow

Thick and strong

Along its winding

Banks and turns,

Fate is your hand,

Redemption is said

To lovingly greet

The weary traveller

When the zenith

Is longingly reached,

A circle of constants,

Parameters and variables,

Circumstance delayed,

The meridian follows

Our solitary surface,

Passing through

Our given place

In the vast universe,

Pathways and poles,

Celestial energy flows

Within love and form,

Echoes of the great path,

The never ending way,

When we become one

With our true existence,

Comprehended psyche,

We can be, journey,

Weave our fibre

Through the tapestry

Of the unknown,

We are everything,

Each movement,

Each moment,

Each convulsion

Of moon, planet,

And burning star,

Encompassed beauty,

Consciousness is dimensional

Non-existence existing,

Expanding, deflating

With the natural

Movements of forever,

Light spreads and colour

Resonates, the world

Becomes limitless,

And I am not afraid

Any more.

Nonsense...

Bliss drizzled deep groves

Of undeniable devotion,

Divinely touching recesses

Of hate, fate, in dire strait.

A psychological state

Beyond the doors of

Perception that swarms

The obsolete tick tock tick

Of T T Time.

Boeotian to the soul,

Ne'er more than whole,

Is this getting droll?

Hautain are my views

On your opinion.

Stimulating as they

Or this may not be

In the eye of the beholder.

Trapped, snared, bamboozled

Beyond breakfast.

Only another hour to go!

Is this another fine mess

You've gotten us in to?

PHEN WESTON

Without A Footprint

Ode to B. G.

Words escape the pages

Without a footprint

Across the peaceful

Sun saturated

English countryside,

Concept and belief,

Teaching and understanding,

Three worlds apart,

Metaphysically together,

Ideas scribed by your hand

Sought out by my mind,

Notions among notions,

Running free, unbound

By their binding,

Without a footprint,

Meaning and impression,

The mind of an artist laid bare

Like a red headed woman drawn

NOTHING BUT THE RAIN

By a protagonist hands,

You are reflected by your

Words, and with each word,

A spectre is reviewed,

And I am in awe,

I will not leave

Footprints on this land.

Defibrillated Love

She was

A shock to my system,

Full of electric passions

Fusing voltage with vigour,

It was a case of

Electromagnetic personalities,

Opposites attract

With inductive impulses,

Yet, she discharged emotions

Like alternating current,

Paroxysm jolts, shifting

With polar moods,

Pylons and polarities,

In the end, there was only

Surges, short circuits, spikes,

Infatuation and power failure.

To W.

Tentative nurturer,
Your strength resounds
In life given from heart,
In wisdom taught prolifically
And daringly blessed upon
The newfound soul,
Goddess supremely loved,
With deep flowing rivers
Of warming replenishment,
How can I define in words
The life you so freely
Give to me with each second
Spent held in your arms,
Love denied subtle winds
For far too long before you,
That even to angels the idea
Vanished into forgotten lore,
Lost literature of lost masters,
Life drawn out of lines
By short strung attentions
Too plagued to really feel,
Life became the hollow shell
Of empty faces, strangers
Filed in unfulfilled cabinets,
How could the world exist

When inside these ghosts

Walks the ghost of me,

To darkness and damnation

I slept away the days,

Until through the sheen

Of such wanton horror

Your light paraded within

Frigid bitter shadows,

Until light was forever and eternal,

Every second that passes

In your seraphim presence

Is an infinite adventure

Outlasting the spiteful hold

Of dying deities,

No being, nor universe,

Could hope to out strive

The boundless aeons of each

Humble second I share with you,

Each plainly given to me openly,

Life becomes a gracious gift

When reinstated through you,

How could I not be in awe?

Lover and saviour so sweet

Words would be too discreet

For gracing what you have given,

And I will love you beyond

Words, worlds or time!

NOTHING BUT THE RAIN

Pont de l'Archevêché

"I went to the Garden of Love,
And saw what I never had seen."
- William Blake

Our love locked

With so many

Hopes and dreams,

One thousand

Thousand destinies,

And so many more,

Some thrive,

Some fade,

The test of time

Will stand

Before us all

And ours will last

Beyond time,

And I will

Love you

Always,

A declaration

Carved in metal,

Locked in place,

For all to see,

The key gently floats

To rest in calming

Perfect waters below

Pont de l'Archevêché,

And I will

Love you

Always.

Can We Sail Away?

Esoteric essence,

I felt you cry again,

Flooding the walkways

Of worlds created

In our darkest yesternight,

Vicariously we love

The surrogate substitute

Of abstruse wanderings,

We kiss recherché moments

With puzzling certainty,

Holding on to those

Impenetrable notions,

And how deeply I wait

For your derivative wants.

Alone in our tryst

Where sorrows adjourn,

Come find me where

I wait for you,

In the rivers we fabricate,

Delusions drown me.

The Victorian Portrait Company

We hang our shame on the wall
For the world to thoughtfully dissect,

A distorted family masterpiece of ill will,
Bitterness and venom coloured sepia,

Is this post-mortem photography?
A thousand autumns of disrelished taboo?

Each moment fractured, fragmented,
Arranged epoch, Frozen forever,

But this is no Disney fairy tale!
There is no happily ever after!

Antipathy, each carte de visite
Is opposition to who we have become,

We hold our place and hold our time,
Defined repugnance framed In rapport,

And who will ever know or judge
When they too adorn walls religiously,

Each household their own daguerreotype,
Their own archetypal family hanging tree,

Can such emotions be digitally restored
Or are we a new kind of American dream?

NOTHING BUT THE RAIN

PHEN WESTON

The Worlds We Create

Here comes the apex of another day,
The vulnerable moments undefined
Where dreamscapes manifest, but cannot stay,

What words often see through my soul's cliché?
Within their night I am lost, soon to find
Here comes the apex of another day,

Every syllable seems to underplay
The significance of a world confined
Where dreamscapes manifest, but cannot stay

Is life malleable like potters' clay?
Dying stars create the hearts of mankind,
Here comes the apex of another day,

These realms progress toward their own decay,
What times come? In our minds they fall behind
Where dreamscapes manifest, but cannot stay,

All there is, was, will be, dwindles away
Until we hold through the unconscious mind
Here comes the apex of another day
Where dreamscapes manifest, but cannot stay.

The Eve Of War

A softer dawn I had never seen
In years as long as the sky burned,
Sweet crimson sparked life with fiery
Presence into the newly forming day,
Mixing ambers and orange with azure
To glorify the morning procession
Of holy pageantry that awaited each
And every person who embraced life,
The paper shop in which I worked
Moved as though the world always turned,
People flustered, in and out, out and in,
As their daily rituals began, work, home,
Home, work, life, wife, husband, children,
Pets, bills, social, sleep, sleep, sleep,
Picking up their morning dose of trouble
In print, strife here, discord there,
Fine pages that spit the world's split face,
Elaborate displays and ceremonies,
The ever marching propaganda machine,
Such pomp and spectacle for words
With so little value and care,
Across the green the children's joy
Echoed, theatrical youth, grandeur
Touched by loud voices, play and life,
Until the prison bells rang, rang, rang,

To steal their minds and educate mice,
Slowly wishing the hours away
Until they could once more stray
Out with friends into the blushing world,
Their secret dens, in secret streets,
Living a secret life only children see,
And adults reminisce about with age,
Parents park, cars, prams, gossip,
"Oh, 'e left 'er" and "they did that,"
The little shreds of diaphanous exchange
That maybe made their small lives
Seem a little better than they thought
They were, or maybe friendships
Blossomed like the budding spring bouquets
That richly enclosed the pastoral scene,
Encasing lemon, indigo, cerise existence,
And above the world birds flew high,
Such grace on winged esse souls
Watching the pocket-sized human race
Go about their daily trace of being,
This scene, a replica of all the land,
Facsimile of carbon life, minute by minute
On such a day as the sky burned
With magnificent hues and the world
Turned and turned anew, moving
On and on, as though life was always one
With nirvana, and would always be
This beautiful, decorative, way…

The Empath

"To her fair works did Nature link
The human soul that through me ran."
- William Wordsworth

It is a strange cursed
Gift to feel the world,
Mother calls emotion,
Sentient compassion,
Accurate sympathy
Strums the harp,
An ability of a poet's soul?
To understand emotive touch,

I feel fiery passions
Burning with midnight oil,
Sense father's loving grip
And protective strength,
And how deeply I'd give to
Understand a mother's bond
With the celestial womb, pure,
Innocent, divinity,

Yet empathy brings coldness,
Bloodshed bleeds, cripples,
Callous corruptibly, I drown
Within confused whirlpools,

Within confused aeons,
What manner of being can
Cause so much pain to its own
Aching heart, not observing,

Chaos overwhelms and I wish
For rested fickle moments
Where feelings fade,
Sensory deprivation,
Sometimes it is as if I am
Feeding from tender hearts,
Vampiric wraith sustained
By electric charge,

I bleed for the world,
I love for the world,
I feel every ounce of myself
Lost in receptive instinct,
It is a cursed gift
That binds me to my species
So lost in their own wants
As not to perceive numen.

But what a gift!
To feel the pulse of life,
Love, hate, peace, fury,
Every heart beats within me!

Tao

The Tao flows,

Evolves

Its presence

Into all things.

It is all things,

And they are it.

Without time

It moves, minute

To minute

Lifetime to lifetime.

I do not know the Tao,

Or claim to.

If I did, it would not be

The Tao.

The eternal

Force that guides,

Governs,

Teaches.

To me,

All beauty

Comes from

The Tao.

It shows me

How life is,

Why I am.

The mysteries

That bind

And merge

In

And out

Of all we are,

And are not.

The Tao is all.

The way.

Sleep Grimalkin

*"The fear of death follows from the fear of life. A
man who lives fully is prepared to die at any time."*
- Mark Twain

Grimalkin sulked and snuck,
Matted fur, feverish night,
The witching hour lay insight,
Mistress soon would raise her head,

She baited the mouse, slithered,
Waiting to pounce and devour,
Only four teeth remained,
But still enough to snap bone,

She purred playfully to herself,
The stench of death snaked
From her throat, violating the air,
She didn't have a single care,

Burrowing deeper still
Into empty pitched darkness,
Camouflaged from everything,
Except the touch of harbingers,

The night felt freshly fresh

Against her ancient bones,
How she loathed the cold,
Insulated she loathed all,

The mouse gently squeaked,
Her ears curiously pricked,
Soon she would have her fun,
Taste the warm redness anew,

Suddenly the air fractured,
Flashed, flared, flailed,
Leaping, she felt her age,
Disdained the world once again,

Before her a kitten stood,
Young innocent faced fun,
Fragmentation of divinity,
How she loathed the youthful,

"I've come for you old grandma"
Glee filled his every word
"You're long past due"
Grimalkin withdrew, into black,

She glared, "I have no time
For nonsense games," snarled,
She wanted dinner before nightly
Burden, drudgery, duty,

NOTHING BUT THE RAIN

"Your work is done old one,
Now I have come," prowess prowled,
"Far beyond your normal years
You have wrongly been enslaved."

Experience told her truths
She long knew, she loathed truth,
But enslavement was an odd
Choice of stubborn words,

How could one be a slave
To time, when it was such
A precious commodity,
She didn't loathe time,

"There is more time than this,"
The kitten calmly, caringly claimed,
Callous the words slammed
Her senior ears, loathing lingered,

Tattered, moth-eaten hair
Stood erect, shivers and shakes,
"Life will be beautiful my friend"
She loathed beautiful too,

The witch stirred, soon the hour
Engulfed, no rest for the wicked,
Was there more than aching bones?
Raspy, her voice caught inside,

Images flowed of younger days,
Before her haggard mistress strayed
And dragged her loathingly
Along her darker path, loathingly,

Playful kitten turned his head
And light illuminated the nearly dead,
Earthly turmoil she would shed,
No longer hallowed to be bled,

"Grimalkin, sweet Grimalkin,
Rest those tired eyes and know
Your time and playful prize,
I am here for you alone."

Grimalkin loathed alone,
But she loathed this long life
Even more when pleasure
Had long since shut its door,

What was she still waiting for?
And Grimalkin bowed her head,
"If there's more to this than dead
Show me kitten your soft, soft bed."

Grimalkin, matted fur and fang,
Rested one final time, shut her eyes,
Gravely and harsh breathing faded,

NOTHING BUT THE RAIN

And gracefully, loathing left,

Grimalkin, queen of cats,
Sat and bathed in endless light,
Basking, she breathed deep,
Loving eternal pleasures, at peace.

4am (The Prequel)

*"How far away the stars seem, and how far is
our first kiss, and ah, how old my heart."*
- William Butler Yeats

The mornings slowly

Darken, faithful hues

Change to drifted shades,

Even August cannot

Hold the coming seasons

From transforming,

But, this does not tame

The tranquility of

Summer dreams,

Only keeps them fresh

For another year, when

Life comes around,

NOTHING BUT THE RAIN

Hush still chimes

Along empty streets

With vanished words,

Racing rats are still,

Oblivious to such an hour,

Dusk's morning pray,

For peaceful rest,

I too wish for noble slumber,

But 4am insidiously came,

And went…

Yet what poetry

Each early morning holds.

ABOUT THE AUTHOR

Phen is a poet and writer from Devon, England. He is currently a mature student, studying for a Bachelor's Degree in English and History at Plymouth University and loving every second. When not studying, writing or working he spends his time with his fiancé wandering, as well as with his children, family and friends.

You can always find him at: http://darknesswarmth.wordpress.com/

Printed in Great Britain
by Amazon.co.uk, Ltd.,
Marston Gate.